LIGHT AND ILLUSION

LIGHT AND

THE HOLLYWOOD

Tom Zimmerman   FOREWORD BY *Robert Stack*

EDITED BY *John Jones*

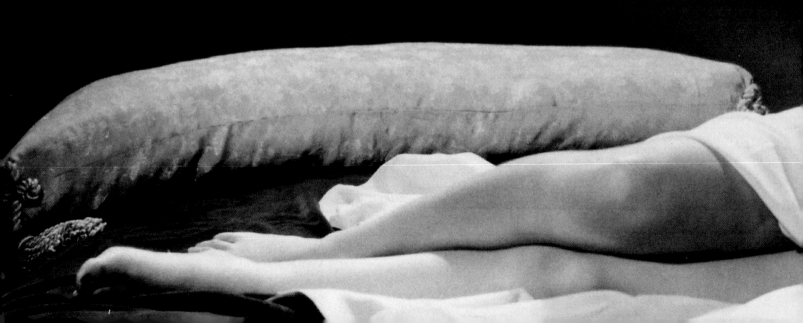

ILLUSION

PORTRAITS OF RAY JONES

Published in the United States of America 1998

Design by Jim Drobka
Typeset in Granjon and Lucida Sans

Imaging and printing by Navigator Press, Pasadena, California

For information, address BALCONY PRESS
512 East Wilson, Glendale, California 91206

Light and Illusion: The Hollywood Portraits of Ray Jones
© John Jones 1998

Library of Congress Catalog Card Number: 97-077841

ISBN 1-890449-00-8

CONTENTS

Robert Stack, 1939

FOREWORD

Ray Jones was one of my best friends, a mentor, fellow duck hunter, and probably the finest still photographer to grace our profession. As a wide-eyed beginner under contract to Universal Studios, Ray took me under his wing and showed me how to make sense of an often senseless business.

He was catnip to the beautiful screen kittens who would line up to be glamourized by Ray Jones' camera. His job was to make Carole Peters into Carole Lombard, Edna Mae into Deanna Durbin, Bernie Schwartz into Tony Curtis and so on....
He was a magician who made us all look the way we wished we looked. I wish that Ray Jones were here today.

Robert Stack, 1998

Gods and Goddesses

WALKED THE EARTH IN HOLLYWOOD sixty years ago, in the mythology of the movies. They walked right through the Great Depression and the worst war the world has ever seen.

Much of what we think of as the glamour of that time comes to us by way of the studio portrait photographers. They used light to create illusion. The stars were real people transformed into myths by the studios. Names were changed, pasts rewritten and always sweetened, faces and bodies made stunning by costumers and retouchers. The movie itself was only a passing story, while the great studio portraits were romanticized ideals caught frozen in time: lasting objects of perfection to hold in your hands.

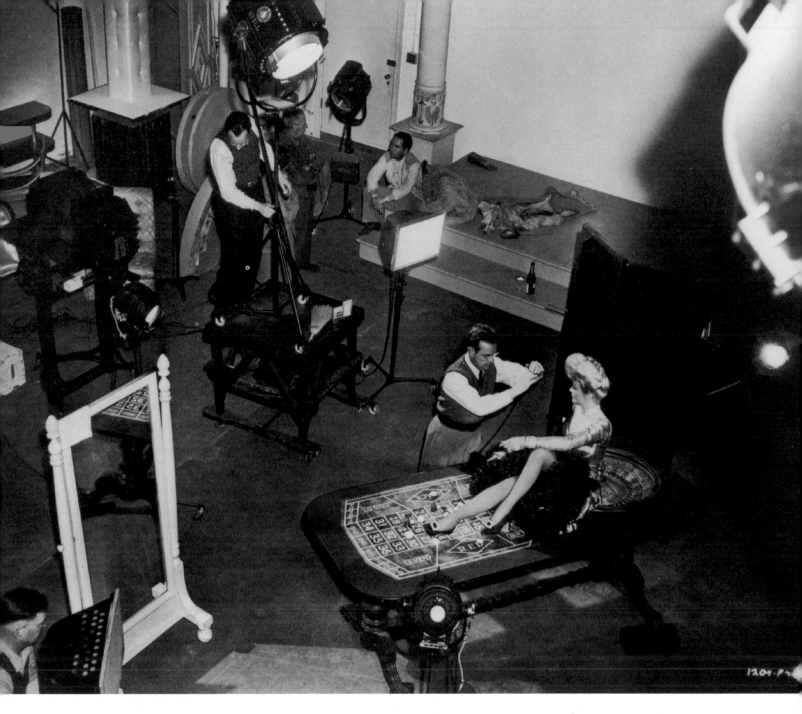

CREATING GLAMOUR

Ray Jones, the chief portrait photographer of Universal Studios from 1935 to 1958, was a master of light and illusion. He worked very hard to create and sustain the Hollywood deities, vital to the transformation of good-looking human beings into what his friend and frequent subject, Robert Stack, called, "glamourized perfection that the audience could go and lose themselves in."[1]

The images cast on the huge screens of downtown palaces and neighborhood theaters obviously played a part in the creation of the otherworldly glamour that

Ray Jones with Marlene Dietrich in Photo Gallery for the 1941 movie, SEVEN SINNERS. *The mirror, Marlene's idea, annoyed photographers. She always wanted to see how she was being posed.*

9

The mode of the moment is military; Deanna Durbin cashes in on it with a striking white broadtail evening cape. Effective style strategy is the wide epaulet top with its stand-up collar that can be detached and worn over high-style suits or afternoon dresses. New husband Vaughn Paul approves the new hairdress; all girls endorse the jewelry—pink tourmaline leaf clip and a pink gold bracelet featuring emerald-cut amethyst, round diamonds and rubies; the Army will sanction the cape, a telling feminine maneuver on the autumn style front

FOR FALL FASHIONS

YOUNG
Mrs. PAUL
PREFERS—

Studio portrait galleries were also responsible for taking the fashion layout photos that ran in the various movie magazines. Deanna Durbin (The Young Mrs. Vaughn Paul) appeared in a five-page spread modeling fall fashions in PHOTOPLAY's October, 1941 issue.

Irene Dunne in a cover photo from the October, 1941 issue of PHOTOPLAY. Jones received credit on the contents page.

was the stock-in-trade of Hollywood. But, on a more personal level, the stars could be brought right into the home. All of the Hollywood portraitists exposed their negatives for publication by the halftone and rotogravure presses of the day. The studios also sent out thousands of portraits every week to fans who asked for the images, perhaps hoping to associate themselves with the Hollywood scene.

Stars' portraits were published in Sunday rotogravure sections all over the country, in fan magazines such as *Motion Picture, Movie Life, Movie Star, Parade, Photoplay, Picture Play, Screenland, Screen Stars,* and, later, the picture magazines such as *Pic and Click*. This was as close to their idols as fans in the 1930s and '40s were ever likely to get.

Ray Jones was one of very few photographers who created these images. Each of the five major—MGM (Loews), Fox, RKO, Warner Brothers, Paramount—and three secondary studios—Universal, Columbia, United Artists—had a chief of the portrait gallery. He would usually be the head of the Still Photos unit, under the control of the Publicity Department.

The Stills Unit was divided into two sections. The Portrait Studio had a chief and one or two photographers who were responsible for taking the glamour portraits used to introduce the studio's newest contract player, to publicize a particular role in a film, to keep the star before the fans, or to transform an actor's image. The Stills Section, with its five to eight photographers, would shoot production photos on picture sets, at costume fittings, out in the world to record scenes to be reproduced on the lot, to cover premieres—or anything else requiring pictures. Other than for magazines and newspapers, the various photos would be used on the movie's advertising posters and lobby cards.[2]

There was no question that the studios recognized the importance of photographs in selling their product. The prevailing attitude of the importance of pictures to the Publicity machine was explained in a 1937 industry publication called "Advertising the Motion Picture." "Photography is at once a prime factor of the motion picture advertiser's subject matter and his surest tool…. Here the copy is, in striking act, the product itself, sampled as frankly as a plugged watermelon."[3]

The "product" was the star or the film. The stars were emblematic of their studios representing a huge investment in time and money. The photographers may have created the photos appearing all over the country, but their work was rarely credited and they remained largely anonymous studio employees.

BUILDING THE STUDIO SYSTEM

Like so much else in United States history, the movies started in the East and moved West. Thomas Edison, the East Coast giant, is beloved in American memory as the inventor of the light bulb, the gramophone, and the motion-picture camera. He was also as hard-headed a businessman as Jacob Astor, Cornelius Vanderbilt, Andrew Carnegie or any of the other financial barons of the late 19th century. In 1909, he was instrumental in organizing the Motion Picture Patents Company. Called "The Trust," it consisted of ten companies holding the majority of patents on both film making and projecting equipment. Either you paid money to Edison and the other members of the Trust, or you didn't get to use their machinery.

Such a lockout was, of course, impossible to maintain. The Independents, as non-Patent companies were called, used European-made equipment and sought out right-to-work states. Escaping Edison's New Jersey base of operations is often cited as the reason film companies came to Los Angeles. The main reason the early film crews arrived, however, was the singular blend of climate, cheap land, wildly varied topography, and the abundance of eclectic architecture to be found in Southern California.

In the East, the miserable weather made expensive, enclosed studios a necessity. The invigorating climate of Los Angeles, by contrast, enabled many silent movies to be shot outdoors on open-air sets covered by muslin to diffuse the brilliant sunlight.

The first impromptu studio in Los Angeles was constructed in 1908 by Francis Boggs of the Selig Company, behind a downtown Chinese laundry near 7th and Olive. The first Hollywood studio was opened in 1911 in a shuttered roadhouse at the corner of Sunset and Gower by the Nestor Company. These were opening shots in a revolution that would crown Los Angeles the new capital of film production.

The Trust was ended by lawsuit in 1915, bringing down the barriers so that new companies could start up. In the new, blooming environment, Russian-born junk dealers could—and did—become moguls. Unknowns from Pennsylvania found themselves sexual icons. Former soldiers went from gofers to directors.

By the early 1920s, order emerged. Eight studios came out of the melee and controlled the industry. They organized the film business into huge, vertically controlled companies that were responsible for a film's production, advertising, distribution, and, often, exhibition.[4]

THE APPRENTICESHIP OF RAY JONES

Ray Jones would enter this potent mix in 1923. He was born in Superior, Wisconsin in 1900. His father, Henry Clay Jones, was a gambler in both business and games of chance. As a result, the Jones finances were mercurial and the family moved often. Ray was the second of four children. He started working after school at nine years old. His job was to sweep and clean the studios and darkroom at the Drysdale-Perry Photographic Studios, Superior's largest photo concern, and one, incidentally, that is still in business. Ray was immediately hooked. The need to help support his family led him to his life's calling.

When Ray was a sophomore at Superior Central High School, and his older brother, Cecil, was a senior, their traveling-salesman father suffered a fatal heart attack. It was a common story early in the century. With the death of their father, the schooling of the oldest boys ended and they had to find steady work.

Ray was fortunate that he was already working part-time on the fringe of the career he had always wanted. He was able to get a full-time position with Drysdale-Perry, going from cleaning, to learning darkroom skills and lighting, and finally to helping photographers in the field.

Jones had just started to take photos for the Studio when the U.S. entered World War I. Initially, he wanted to join the military, but at seventeen was underage and needed his mother's permission. Anna Jones was barely making it as a seamstress. She explained to Ray that his paycheck was vital to keeping the family together. So he joined his brother, doing war work at home as a welder for the Superior Ship Building Company.

Drysdale-Perry Photographic Studios, Superior, Wisconsin, 1932: Ray Jones' entry into the world of photography. (Photographer unknown)

After the Armistice, Jones returned to Drysdale-Perry to continue preparing for a photo career. Because Drysdale-Perry was a major commercial photography studio, he was able to learn all aspects of the photo business. Jones not only became a proficient technician, he adapted to taking interior portraits, exterior scenery and architectural shots. He learned all he could about the properties of film, chemicals, and the cumbersome 4 x 5" and 8 x 10" view cameras that were the standard of commercial studios at the time. Considering his later work, it is surprising that in Superior he specialized in outdoor shots.

By 1923, Ray Jones was beginning to feel dulled by the work he was doing for Drysdale-Perry. As he later recalled, "I left Superior in favor of Hollywood simply because it was a natural step. I realized that I had gone as far as I could where I was working. In casting about for a logical place to go, it was natural that I would think of Hollywood. It's the one place in the world where there is no limit to a photographer's opportunities."[5]

Jones arrived in downtown Los Angeles at the Southern Pacific train station at the foot of Fifth Street and set out for Hollywood. His first job, with his future long-time employer, Carl Laemmle's Universal Studio, was not even close to the exalted Portrait Department: Ray started his movieland career taking pictures of studio banquets. He soon left this to operate a stills concession with another photographer at the Mack Sennett Studios. At that time, Sennett had no stills department and the necessary pictures were taken by concessionaires who worked only when needed.

Alys Murrell's ornate headdress, rather than A.W. Witzel's lighting scheme, sets her apart from the background (date unknown). A.W. Witzel opened his first photo gallery in Los Angeles in 1896. By 1925, Witzel had three studios, one downtown and a very busy one on Hollywood Boulevard. He closed all of his studios around 1930 and disappeared from photography.

Mary Miles Minter was a major silent film actress whose career ended when she was implicated in the murder of director William Desmond Taylor in 1922. This A.W. Witzel portrait (date unknown) is typical of the early star shots. The lighting is quite flat, the attitude wholesome. The props are simple and far darker than the subject, who stands out in her white dress and pale skin.

BUILDING THE STAR SYSTEM

Like sports, the movie business would eventually get endless free advertising by periodicals and newspapers eager to feed the interests and fantasies of their readers. At first, the players were anonymous. Published pictures of them were labeled "The Biograph Girl," "Little Mary," or "Bronco Billy." Under the Patents Trust, filmmakers were reluctant to feature any actors' names for fear individual fame would bring demands for larger salaries. Also, the movies were only one- or two-reelers, cranked out rapidly and shown at the local nickelodeon.

Moviegoers were seen as loyal to specific companies, not to stars. So who cared who was in them?

The fans, that's who. Their interest, expressed through thousands of letters, gave Carl Laemmle an idea. He knew the star was always a driving force in plays and vaudeville. In 1910, he hired away Florence Lawrence, who was known only as "The Biograph Girl," and began featuring her in movies under her own name.

Laemmle was a great believer in advertising. He found that, while he had to pay Lawrence a higher salary than she had been receiving from Biograph, he was also able to charge higher rental rates for her films. Before this time, movies were often rented by the foot rather than by individual films.

The rising of the star system made household names of Florence Turner (formerly "The Vitagraph Girl"), Maurice Costello, Arthur Johnson, and comedian John Bunny. Soon it would shine with the additions of Mary Pickford and Charlie Chaplin.

Famous Players-Lasky opened the first studio-owned portrait gallery in 1920 or '21. Before this, photos were the responsibility of the actor. By the end of the decade, all the majors, and even some of the smaller studios, had on-lot stills galleries, established to exercise company control over the presentation of their two biggest assets—movies and stars.

The introduction of the Stills Department was part of the general trend toward integrated vertical organization that characterized the emerging major studios in the early 1920s. Top stars, Lillian Gish, for example, would spend upwards of $10,000 a year on photographs—before the Stills Departments. The studio galleries put an end to the lucrative business of New York studios such as Apeda, Mishkin, and Underwood and Underwood, as well as the downtown Los Angeles firms, A.W. Witzel, Nelson Evans and others.

The first set stills were often taken by the cinematographer. D.W. Griffith's great photographer, Billy Bitzer, kept a still camera near his movie camera and did two jobs at once. As the stillsman became a more independent entity, many skilled lensmen migrated to Hollywood. Men who would later make their reputations as cinematographers often started out taking portraits and stills. James Wong Howe's photos of Mary Miles Minter were instrumental in building his career as an cinematographer. Karl Struss, already a major name in fine art photography, came to Hollywood in 1919 at the behest of Cecil B. DeMille to photograph Gloria Swanson in *Male and Female*. He was followed by Edward Curtis, who had made his reputation publishing the twenty-volume *The North American Indian*.

Edward Curtis' "set still" of Roman Navarro, c. 1924. Though he worked on many silent film sets, Curtis will always be remembered first for his twenty-volume study of THE NORTH AMERICAN INDIAN.

Edwin Bower Hesser portrait of Helen Ferguson, c. 1920. Hesser left Hollywood for the color photographic department of the NEW YORK TIMES *in 1929, after the studios opened their own galleries. Hesser is best remembered for his* EDWIN BOWER HESSER'S ARTS *magazine, published throughout the 1920s and featuring studio and outdoor shots of nudes done in the Pictorial style.*

15

Jean Rogers, c. 1938. This is a classic 1930s glamour shot. Jean Rogers' blond hair called for a dark background, so the lights were set away from the wall or fixed with directional shoots. The key light is set high to the front to illuminate the face and jacket and to create the dramatic shadows from the false eyelashes and the "butterfly effect" under her nose. An overhead light is set to outline facial features, illuminate the hair, and bring up the highlights on the jacket's sequins.

The early photos from Witzel, Evans, and Edwin Bower Hesser were not ground-breaking images. They were quite typical of the theatrical pictures of the era. The composition was generally simple, with few props, flat lighting, soft focus and demure clothing. The style of the iconographic portraits associated with the Golden Age of Hollywood developed gradually. The more impressive work involving intricate lighting styles would come later. It would be, along with the extensive use of photographs in the promotion of the city, one of Los Angeles's two significant contributions to the history of photography.

The 1920s and '30s saw a tremendous photographic debate that did not revolve around portrait style, but rather on focus. Pictorialism, the soft-focus, painterly, consciously "artistic" approach to photography popular since the turn of the century, was increasingly being attacked as "fuzzygraphs" by proponents of straight, unmanipulated photography such as Alfred Stieglitz and Paul Strand in New York and Edward Weston, Ansel Adams and the other members of Group F64 [6] in California. In the Hollywood Stills Studios, the definite winner was the straight approach.

The style of Hollywood portrait that developed during the 1920s was pioneered by Edward Steichen in *Vanity Fair* magazine. The props in the photos remained minimal, but the lighting changed radically and the stars' images became overtly sexual. The soft-focus, romantic pictures by Witzel, Baron deMeyer, Edwin Bower Hesser, Arnold Genthe, Alfred Chaney Johnston, and James Abbe became archaic. Under the skilled hands of Ray Jones, George Hurrell, Clarence Sinclair Bull, John Engstead, Elmer Fryer, Whitey Schafer, Bob Coburn, and Ernest Bachrach, stars and contract players were transformed from the ordinary to the hyper-glamourous. [7]

16

As the late 1920s merged into the '30s, the portraiture so emblematic of the Golden Age of Hollywood emerged as a distinct iconographic style. The new photographic approach featured expressive "Rembrandt" lighting that created striking shadows molding the face and body. New sources of illumination were developed, including overhead boom lights that could be used to highlight either head and shoulders or the backdrop. The introduction of panchromatic film — which registered the full color spectrum on black and white film — helped produce a fuller tonal range in prints. After the photographers had worked their magic with lights, the 8 x 10" negatives were handed off to the retouchers. What emerged was a very highly stylized portrait of something that was not entirely of this earth. It was a portrait of a star. [8]

Ray and Raella Jones, 1932

RAY JONES AT UNIVERSAL

Ray Jones spent the 1920s perfecting his craft and, incidentally, courting and, in 1929, marrying, Raella Raye. Jones had been an outdoor specialist in Superior, and had had to learn the trade of the stillsman and portraitist in Hollywood. He spent time at Fox, Samuel Goldwyn, and Paramount before joining Universal as Jack Freulich's assistant in the Portrait Gallery in 1931.

Jones left to head the Still Department at Fox in 1933. After a year, he went freelance and took pictures for Columbia and Paramount, then was hired as Freulich's replacement to head the Still Department at Universal in 1935. A key element in his hiring was the spectacular work he did on Cecil B. DeMille's *Cleopatra*. Jones was joined at various times in the portrait gallery by Ed Estabrook, Roman Freulich (Jack's brother) and William Walling. He also had the opportunity to hire his younger brother, Eddie Jones, to shoot production stills.

As with the other majors, Universal's stills section was under the control of the Publicity Department. This played to Ray Jones' particular strength. He was able to work with the publicists to create the image a new contract player or star needed, depending on the direction of his or her career. But, however happy Jones was to be back at the Studio where he had started twelve years earlier, he had arrived at a bad time.

Universal nearly went bankrupt in 1935. Carl Laemmle was forced to take out a loan to keep the studio afloat; he put up his controlling company stock as collateral. When the loan came due, Laemmle did not have the money, and the debt was called in. J. Cheever Cowdin of Wall Street's Standard Capital Corporation now controlled Universal. The company had already lost its 315-theater chain. With the now austere regime

Poupée Andriot played one of the French girls in ALL QUIET ON THE WESTERN FRONT. *It was Universal's premiere release in 1931 and one of Jones' first assignments after landing his job at the Studio.*

17

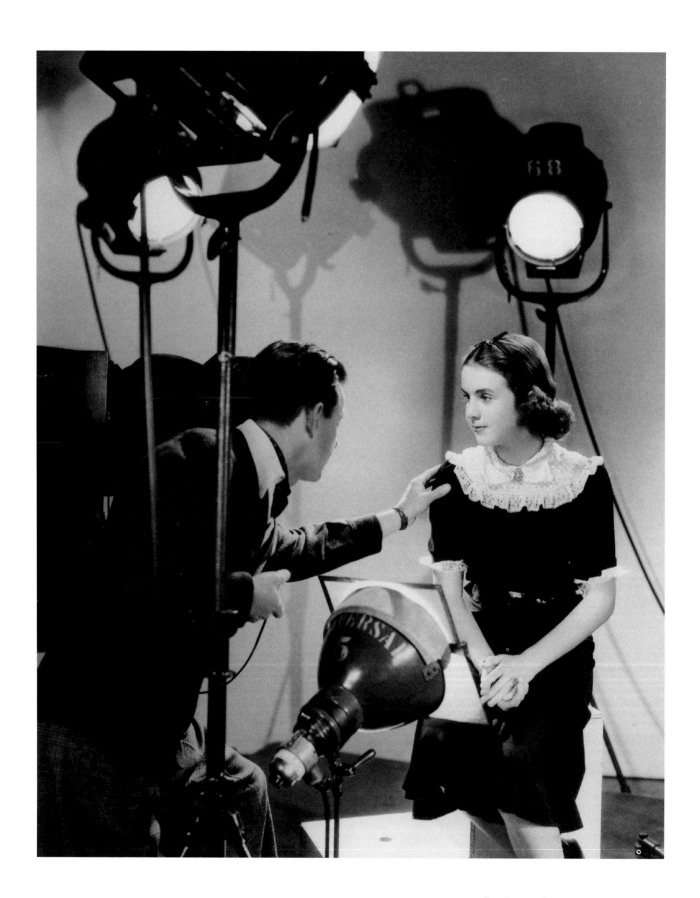

Ray Jones and Deanna Durbin in the Gallery, 1936

under new production chief
Charles Rogers, Universal
concentrated on fare for the
"subsequent-run" houses
in cities and independent
theaters in small towns.
These included serials, news-
reels, B features, and a return
to the company's monster
movies of years earlier.

Composite sheet of Yvonne DeCarlo pinups, 1945.

This meant that Jones had few established contract
stars to shoot. Lew Ayres and Margaret Sullavan had
been with the Studio for years, but were soon to leave.
They were replaced by teenager Deanna Durbin, whose
contract MGM had let slide in favor of Judy Garland.
Durbin was the last-minute addition to a 1936 B movie
called *Three Smart Girls*, which became a huge hit and
established Durbin's career. The even greater success of
the follow-up, *One Hundred Men and a Girl*, made her
the queen of the Universal lot and finally helped move
the Studio back into the black.

The studio portraits were striking because of
the familiarity that developed between Ray Jones and
the stars during years of association. Ray Jones first
photographed Deanna Durbin as an innocent teenager.
As her career developed, he began shooting her as a
mature young woman. Yvonne DeCarlo came to
Universal after Paramount failed to renew her option.
Jones began by taking pinups of the former dancer.
Her big break came with *Salome, Where She Danced*
in 1945. She posed for hundreds of harem-girl pictures
for this and subsequent "costumer" roles. In 1947 she
graduated into film noir femme fatale roles, and again
photos fed the publicity machine. Maria Montez, on the
other hand, never strayed far from costumed, native-girl

*This 1945 shot of Yvonne DeCarlo is from the
same session as the series of eight shown above;
however, this picture showed a prominent crotch
and too much breast, so it was out of bounds for
general publication.*

19

1322-179AA

20

An excellent example of Jones' technique, this photograph has Maria Montez lying on an often-used prop. The bed appears in many photos, covered with varying sheets, pillows, or blankets as the shot dictated. The white costume stands out perfectly from the darker props and wall. The rectilinear nature of the pillows and bed accentuates Maria's curves. Her face and body are angled into the key light. Raising both arms also raises her breasts, making them both fuller and more accentuated by the lights. The costume is perfectly arranged to conceal both the navel and inner thigh while hinting at both. The lighting effect on the back wall comes from a cucoloris: an attachment placed over the light to create an effect on a flat surface (date unknown).

parts. Her range as an actress was rather minimal, but she filled out a sarong in a most spectacular fashion and was always the prototypical movie star in her portraits.

Sittings could last an hour or all day, requiring costumers, makeup artists and hair stylists. Jones would work the huge view camera required to house an 8 x 10" negative, while his assistants manipulated the lights and backdrops according to his directions. It was Jones' responsibility to soothe the stars, find their best angles, adjust the lights to bring out their most flattering features, and—finally—take the picture. Once the darkroom technicians developed and proofed the film, the key images were selected and sent off to the retouchers. Their job was to clean up any flaws in the star. Facial blemishes, bags under the eyes, excess stomach, leg or arm imperfections, and (due to the edicts of the production code office) women's cleavage—all evaporated.

Because of its short star list, Universal was very active in using freelance and loaned stars in their films. James Stewart, Irene Dunne, Claudette Colbert, and Carol Lombard all did films at Universal and posed for Ray Jones' camera. The portrait studio was also responsible for the buildup of new contract players. Photos were put before the public either to start a buzz or to test their appeal.

The only kind of sitting that depressed Jones was when a woman who obviously had no hope of a film career was sent over by someone in the front office. He tried his best to give her a nice picture, knowing it was just a souvenir for someone who had been used as a dalliance.

Paramount Stills Department head A.L. Whitey Schafer's satiric 1940 photo sums up all of the elements that could not be included in stills or movies.

Jill Dennett, 1934

Jones in the Gallery working with Maria Montez, 1943

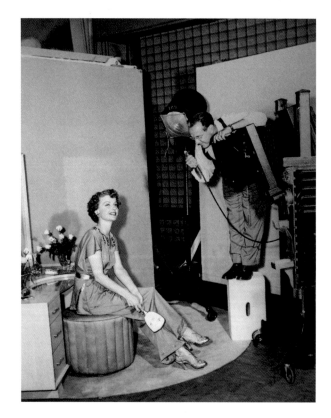

Ann Sheridan in a vanity set constructed in the Portrait Studio. Jones is standing on an "apple box," about to press the cable release attached to his view camera. Next to the camera is the portable carrier holding pre-loaded sheets of 8 x 10" film (1949).

All of the work was carried out in the Stills Building on the Universal lot. Ray Jones was the head of the stills operation and the 54 people who worked there. His portrait gallery was a large space with an eighteen-foot ceiling on the east end of the building. Lights, backdrops, and the huge 8 x 10" view camera on the 12-foot-high rail system Jones developed were permanent residents. Each of the three dressing rooms had a specific purpose. One was for body makeup, the second for face and hair, and the third for clothes. Several grips would work each of the shoots, helping Jones position the lights and camera. The Properties Department supplied whatever special items were needed for a portrait.

The rest of the building contained the production stills office, a storage room for the equipment of the five or six photographers employed at any given time, and the ancillary offices of the photo publicity operation. The darkroom where technicians developed the negatives shot in the gallery and on the set was next to the finishing rooms, where the film and prints were washed and dried. From there they were taken to a sorting room where they were divided according to destination. One pile was for fans, another for general publication, and others for exclusive use of a single image for a particular magazine. In a separate room next to the Gallery, several retouchers worked over the 8 x 10" negatives, erasing any flaws and perfecting, always perfecting.[9]

OPPOSITE

Maria Montez and Jon Hall were another of the couples who kept Universal in business in the 1940s. Here they are featured in an advertising still for COBRA WOMAN *(1943), posing with a snake prop brought into the Portrait Studio and placed on one of the portable risers. The key light is placed to the left, with fill lights from above, right center and right. The key light placement emphasizes Hall's face and the snake's head, as well as Maria's jawline and breasts. Some retouching was done to both of the stars' faces and to Maria's left thigh. Her right breast was also worked on to make it look higher.*

1310-119BB

Another aspect of Jones' job as chief portraitist was to carry out any unique demands from the Publicity Department. One such case was the buildup of Meg McClure. She was a recently signed starlet who had been assigned a part in the 1949 film noir, *Criss Cross*. Jones had already been successful in the transformation of Yvonne DeCarlo from an exotic Technicolor costume star of movies—such as *Slave Girl* and *Salome*—into a modern woman. Meg McClure not only needed a buildup as the new girl at the studio; she also needed a new stage name. Her real name was Gene Thorpe. She had used the name Gene Roberts when under contract at MGM and Fox. Studio execs at Universal did not like the name but had not come up with a new one before filming began on *Criss Cross*. She was therefore listed on the cast sheet as "Miss X."

This gave Universal publicist Harry Freidman an idea. He placed articles in the fan magazines urging people to write in with a name for Miss X. The letters arrived by the thousands. Jones, who had been busy making portraits of Meg in her costume for *Criss Cross*, was dispatched to shoot her in front of the mail room. So the studio got one type of publicity in the urge to name and another in the result of the contest. Photographs were key to both ends of the campaign.[10]

The studio even created photo opportunities from Ray Jones' road trips. Local press and national magazines covered Jones's trip to San Francisco in 1939 to photograph the dancers of Paris' Folies Bergère, appearing at the Golden Gate International Exposition on San Francisco's Treasure Island. While at the Fair, Jones also took pictures of the Fair Theme Girl, the indefatigable Zoe Dell Lantis. Dressed as the Pirate Girl and undaunted by any challenge, she was the most photographed woman in America for the two years of the Exposition.

Zoe Dell Lantis grew up in rural Oregon. She came to San Francisco to join the city's ballet company. In 1937, she was just twenty when a publicity job for the upcoming Golden Gate International Exposition opened up. She soon became the official Theme Girl of the Fair. Because it took place on Treasure Island, Zoe dressed as a pirate. She visited 47 states (Florida excepted), Canada, and Mexico to publicize the Fair. Zoe was that great archetype: the spirited all-American girl. No challenge too great, nothing too intimidating. For the two years of the Fair she rode horses and elephants, did flips with Native American dancers in Santa Fe, and jumped seven feet over a 900-foot deep part of the Grand Canyon all in high heels. When the Fair was over and she hung up her pirate costume, Zoe became a corporate pilot. (Photographer unknown)

OPPOSITE
Meg McClure, c. 1943, holding mail addressed to "Miss X, Criss-Cross Company," the results of Harry Freidman's publicity campaign.

25

Elyse Knox gets tummy flattened by Ray Jones in the first step of posing for pin-up. Curves must be in the right places.

Dress, hair-do are most important points in pin-up, Jones believes. Here Elyse's coiffure and hips get the final touch.

Long curve of the girl's back is accentuated by Jones as he tucks gown under hips. Only props are backdrop and table.

Ray Jones, behind his camera, directs top lights closer to his subject. His Hollywood suspenders are less garish than most.

"Cross light from the left!" calls Jones, waving dramatically. He invented this tremendous camera mechanism in 1937.

Final shot. Mugging grotesquely, Jones keeps girl's attention during the final few seconds before clicking his camera.

Ray Jones' approach to portraits evolved over his career. The Depression-driven '30s called for larger-than-life perfection in the depiction of stars. The glamour portraits of the 1930s and '40s were intended as fantasies: golden fantasies of perfect people created by the imagination of the great studio photographers and their army of retouchers. The democratizing of World War II and the leveling of the '50s gradually brought a less dramatic, more straightforward view of the stars. Jones' aim was always to work with the Publicity Department to promote the star or film in the prevailing portrait style. As Jones noted, "Glamour photos are a business. Let's face it, they're made for only one purpose: to sell movies."[11]

Jones always stressed the power of creative illumination techniques. One of his favorite quotations was that the "camera has only one eye." In other words, pictures are only two-dimensional. But this could be overcome by the judicious application of light. He argued, "The secret of good portraits is getting the illusion of the third dimension into your pictures. The lens gives you height and width. You have to put depth into your pictures with lights."[12]

26

The photographer laid out his approach in an article for International Photographer. After noting that the miniature informal photos that were just coming into use in 1938 did not have "the depth of color, the proper background effects" obtainable in a studio with large-format cameras, the photographer noted his "Four Rules for a Successful Portrait Sitting":

SPEAKING OF PICTURES . . .

. . . THESE SHOW BEST PIN-UP PHOTOGRAPHER'S TECHNIQUE

Most Hollywood still photographers are good at pin-ups. But Universal's Ray Jones, the winner of this year's Academy Award for the best pin-up picture, is just a little better. On these pages Jones illustrates his special technique with Starlet Elyse Knox. Unlike many of his colleagues who try to exaggerate the lure of an actress by posing her in a maze of gadgets, he concentrates on the girl's particular attractions and carefully emphasizes them with minimum of props. He turns out a picture that is in good taste but still manages to get its peculiar message across. A firm believer in the long-standing Hollywood tradition that the still photographer can make or break a rising star, Ray Jones specializes in the glamor portraits that make the best pin-ups.

A meticulous craftsman, Jones supervises every detail of make-up, hair-do and dress, sometimes even has a drink with his model to help her relax for the tedious posing. Finally, when subject and lights are exactly arranged, he climbs up behind his massive camera (see opposite page) and photographs the actress in the split second when she unconsciously reveals her most characteristic charm.

Jones attributes his expert sense of timing to his practice in photographing babies 22 years ago in Superior, Wis. "You can't stop and ask movie stars how they want their pictures taken," he says. "That's the way it is with photographing babies, especially the ones about 6 months old." It is often necessary to work with a pin-up model for hours before actually taking her picture, but Ray Jones is a patient man.

RESULT OF AN HOUR'S DIRECTION AND POSING IS THIS PORTRAIT OF ELYSE KNOX

Life magazine ran an essay on Jones' style in their May 27, 1944 issue. ©TIME, INC.

First, that all poses must be in keeping with the dramatic background that each subject occupies in the scheme of life;

Second, that the photographer must have a thorough knowledge of the characteristics and mental attitude of the subject;

Third, that the background must be in keeping with the general coloring or 'aura' of each individual who faces the camera;

Fourth, that there must be a feeling of mutual confidence and lack of restraint between the photographer and his 'victim.'[13]

In a decidedly not-for-publication snapshot, Jones captured Marlene Dietrich, John Wayne, Broderick Crawford, and Mischa Auer goofing around before their formal sitting for SEVEN SINNERS (1941).

Ann Blyth was one of the many stars who shared a "mutual confidence" with Jones. She remembers that "Ray's portrait sessions were usually an all-day marathon." The actress would arrive in the morning, trying to prepare herself for the session. The photographer's first job was to set the mood for the sitter. While George Hurrell played lots of music and jumped maniacally about the room, Blyth recalls that Jones "had a way of putting his subject at ease with a kind word or a quip."[14] Rhonda Fleming also remembers being relaxed by Ray's conversation. She also loved music: for their sessions, the record player was in constant use.

Jones was never one to fuss aimlessly about the gallery. He had a definite design for the pictures he wanted, one based on his vision of how best to photograph the subject. The plentiful memos from the Publicity Department explaining the proposed audience for the pictures had to be taken into account as well. Arlene Dahl was always in awe of how Jones could turn directives into photos. She recalled that Jones' charm and personality, as well as his ability "to truly paint with light," made him "one of my favorite photographers."[15]

In 1953 John Gavin was fresh out of the Navy and decided to give acting a try after his friend, Brian Foy, asked him to be in a naval movie about the Korean War. Gavin was eventually signed by Universal and sent to Ray's gallery for portraits. The new actor immediately relaxed as Jones asked him about his life and spoke candidly about the Hollywood system.

Gavin, like former Marine Hugh O'Brien, particularly liked that, in his first and subsequent sessions, Jones always explained what he was doing and why it was necessary to ask him to pose as he did.

John Gavin in one of the photos Jones took for the veteran's mother, 1953

Robert Stack played opposite Deanna Durbin in FIRST LOVE *(1939), where he gave Deanna Durbin her first screen kiss.*

Producer A.C. Lyles knew Jones when they were both at Paramount in 1934. He always thought Ray, unlike some of his counterparts, was as adept at photographing men as women.[16] Something as simple as explaining the mechanics of what he was doing may have been one of the reasons Jones got so much from his male subjects.

Gavin also recalled the kindness Ray showed him in shooting several photos of the new actor in his naval uniform for his mother. He had spent thirteen months on the aircraft carrier Princeton in Korean waters, as the Assistant Air Combat Intelligence Officer, and had never had a chance to get any portraits. A seaman's phrase occurred to Gavin as he watched Jones at work: "In the Navy, when a captain was in control, we said he was 'in command of his bridge.' That's how Ray always impressed me in his gallery. He knew what he wanted and how to get it."[17]

Robert Stack came to Universal in 1938 and quickly found more than a photographer in Ray Jones. "He was my confidante," the actor remembers. "He understood that I was a complete neophyte and kind of became a big daddy to me." Stack had no formal training as an actor, and certainly knew nothing of studio

Ray Jones and Robert Stack were frequent hunting companions (1941).

politics. Jones clued him in on how to deal with the camera and told him how the studio operated. "Acting is a very vulnerable profession," Stack recalled, "especially when you're just starting out. It can also be very brutal. But Ray told me, 'anytime you've got a problem, just come on in.' And I did."

Jones and Stack became close friends. They often went duck hunting at a lodge with groups that included Clark Gable and sporting-goods king Alex Kerr. When they were on the lot, Jones was Stack's favorite photographer. The actor felt one of Ray's strengths was his ability to make his subjects comfortable. The sessions for men were not as lengthy as those for women. "There wasn't much delicacy in taking pictures of a guy. The range of emotions you tried to bring out in those days was pretty limited," Stack noted. He was always

Wall of Anne Frank's house with Jones' photo of Deanna Durbin, Robert Stack and Franchot Tone from NICE GIRL, *1941. In a diary entry for July 11, 1942, Anne Frank wrote, "Our little room looked very bare at first with nothing on the walls; but thanks to Daddy who had brought my picture postcards and film-star collection on beforehand, and with the aid of paste pot and brush I have transformed the walls into one gigantic picture. This makes it look much more cheerful." (Photographer unknown)*

impressed with the results. "It was a time when the boy or girl next door was not the answer. People were glamourized, made to look better than they really were. A larger-than-life image was projected. The job of those masters in the still galleries was to make the product better than it actually was. They had to sell the stars."[18]

Robert Stack remembers well the exalted position of movie stars during the Golden Age of Hollywood. He agreed with Carole Lombard that it was like being a member of a club. Entrance to the club started with the stills gallery on the studio lot. However impressive stars may have looked on the big screen, to Stack, "It was the stills gallery that made them gods and goddesses." The image that was created may have consisted of equal parts smoke and mirror, but it had an extraordinary grip on people's imaginations.

The hold the deities had on their fans was worldwide, even infiltrating a carefully concealed bedroom in Amsterdam during World War II. On Anne Frank's wall were several photos she had collected to brighten up her captive life. The Dutch royal family was there, as were the English princesses. Also on her wall were photos of stars from the mythical domain of Hollywood. Up at the top of the display was a Ray Jones portrait of Robert Stack with his frequent collaborator, Deanna Durbin.[19]

OSCARS FOR PHOTOGRAPHERS

The Academy of Motion Pictures Arts and Sciences decided in 1941 that it had done precious little to celebrate the men who had produced the photographs so primary to selling Hollywood's image. Universal's Head of Publicity, John LeRoy Johnson, had the initial idea to create a photo display featuring the best Hollywood stills, based on the annual exhibit of the Hollywood Still Cameraman's Association.

He convinced the Academy to curate and present the Hollywood Studios' Still Photography Exhibit. Eight classifications were chosen, as were judges from the Associated Press, *Life* and *Look*, cinematographer Gregg Toland, and all four of L.A.'s and several other daily newspapers. The call for submissions was put out to all photographers working for the Hollywood Studios. Eventually 636 entries arrived from 59 stillsmen. Over 500 photos were accepted and displayed at the Academy Review Theater in Hollywood from April 14–27, 1941. The brochure noted, "This program has been established by the Academy to bring long deserved greater recognition to the still cameramen and to advance their fine art in the interest of motion pictures." After closing in Los Angeles, the collection traveled to the Museum of Modern Art in New York, and around the country. Parts of it were even exhibited in Australia.

The Academy mounted new shows in 1942 and 1943, stopping only when World War II intervened. A pinup category was added in those years, given the interests — honed by Hollywood — of the era. The final show was held in 1947, with the prints exhibited in the lobby of the Columbia Broadcasting Studio.

30

Universal released this photo of Ray Jones and his two first-prize winning images of Durbin and Dietrich during the Motion Picture Academy exhibit in 1941.

Award for the Most Popular Photograph of the 1941 Academy Awards Stills Exhibit, for Jones' photo of Deanna Durbin. The award was selected by vote of all attendees of the initial Hollywood showing. (All photos this page by Tom Zimmerman)

RIGHT

Best of Show award for the 1942 Stills Exhibit, for Jones' picture of John Wayne

1941 and 1942 gold medals for the Academy Awards Stills Exhibit

Up against the best photographers in the entire film industry, Ray Jones' was honored at all four of the Academy photo exhibits. He was awarded one of the two awards—a Gold Medal or a Certificate of Merit—in each of the shows. On top of this, he was awarded the "Most Popular of Show" statue in 1941 by visitors to the exhibit, for a portrait of Deanna Durbin in a Western outfit taken at a private ranch in the San Fernando Valley. The next year, he won the "Best of Show" award voted by the entire judging committee for a portrait of John Wayne. The portrait was innovative in its lack of retouching of facial creases. It is indicative of how many exclusive deals were made for publication of studio photos that over 100 of the 185 portraits taken of Durbin on the day at the ranch were printed. The one in the exhibit was simply the photographer's favorite.[20]

World War II meant changes for Jones. He again tried to join the service, but he was a family man in his early 40s by this time. Lacking a high-school diploma, he was also ineligible for officers training. Instead, he organized and operated an Army Signal Corps photo studio on the Universal lot. He also took some of the most popular pinups of the war. Especially in demand was his work with Maria Montez, Ramsey Ames, Yvonne DeCarlo, and Jean Parker.

PORTRAIT OF MARLENE DIETRICH

Academy of Motion Picture Arts & Sciences
Gold Medal Winner

BEST ACTION PORTRAIT, 1941

PORTRAIT OF DEANNA DURBIN

Academy of Motion Picture Arts & Sciences
Gold Medal Winner

BEST NOVELTY STILL, 1941

Also voted *Most Popular of Show* by attendees

PORTRAIT OF JOHN WAYNE

Academy of Motion Picture Arts & Sciences
Gold Medal Winner

BEST MALE PORTRAIT, 1942

Also voted *Best of Show* by the judging committee

PORTRAIT OF DEANNA DURBIN

Academy of Motion Picture Arts & Sciences
Gold Medal Winner

BEST FEMALE PORTRAIT, 1942

PORTRAIT OF RAMSEY AMES

Academy of Motion Picture Arts & Sciences
Gold Medal Winner

BEST PINUP, 1943

PORTRAIT OF LUCILLE BALL

Academy of Motion Picture Arts & Sciences
Certificate of Merit

FEMALE PORTRAIT, 1947

Marjorie Main and Percy Kilbride, MA AND PA KETTLE, *1949. The duo did eight Ma & Pa Kettle films.*

THE END OF THE STUDIO SYSTEM

All of the eight major studios made huge profits during the war. Once it was over, Universal again faced major change. This time it was a merger with International Pictures, which featured A-list films made by independent producers. So, Universal made the decision to can its B-movie units, a disaster, as it turned out. By 1948, the studio was forced to close down for a short time. It reopened to again concentrate on the B-level fare that had been its forte for so long.

Abbott and Costello were the first number-one box office attraction in Universal's long history. The "Abbott and Costello Meet…" series sustained the team's popularity after the war. They were joined by Ma and Pa Kettle and, later, Francis the Talking Mule. All these films were simply produced, assembly-line comedies.

Ray Jones continued to shoot whatever the studio needed. The post-war portraiture style was considerably different from the iconographic approach of the Depression years. The stars were now publicized as ordinary people who just happened to be extraordinarily good-looking. By the 1950s, color was becoming increasingly popular. Jones mastered its use, as he did the strobe units that were starting to replace the huge stationary studio lights.

The stars were no longer depicted as deities come to earth. The pseudo-documentary approach to Hollywood pioneered by *Life* magazine led to a much lower-key style of portraiture. New stars, such as Tony Curtis and Rock Hudson, and their movies, still needed building up and introduction to the public. The style of these portraits was modern in its sharp focus, but showed a return to the flat—illuminating rather than molding—light of the 1920s.

Donald O'Connor and Patricia Medina, with Francis the Talking Mule, 1949. There were seven Francis comedies produced during the '50s.

38

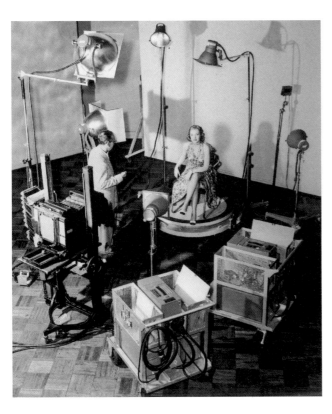

By the mid-1950s, strobe lights had replaced the hot stationary lights in Jones' studio.

Glamour was losing out to a snapshot aesthetic by the mid-1950s. Jones was still using the massive 8 x 10" view camera, but was trying to make a more candid, less posed image. Here the lighting is all key light from the front with a little fill. The point is to sell Mamie Van Doren's sexuality, thus the push-up bra and the extreme angle of her shoulders to raise her breasts. Cocking her right hip accentuates the curve. Leaning against the linear juke box makes her curves more evident as well as appealing to the youth culture that was Mamie's chief audience (1953).

Arlene Dahl starred in DESERT LEGION *with Alan Ladd, 1953*

The number of movies being released by Universal declined with the advent of television, so Jones sometimes found himself with time on his hands. During one such period in 1953, he was sent out to help publicize *Desert Legion*. He was in Minneapolis for the film when he took time to photograph Grace Stimson, who had won a contest for the privilege. The event was, of course, covered in the local papers, including not only the portrait of Stimson, but Jones' now historic glamour shots of Marlene Dietrich, Rhonda Fleming, Susan Hayward, Lucille Ball, and hometown girl Arlene Dahl.[21]

The studio system was a short-lived entity. The eight major studios, controlling the vast majority of film production as well as the most lucrative theaters, had emerged in the 1920s. By the 1950s, the combination of television, the Supreme Court's Paramount decision ordering the studios to divest themselves of their theater chains, and the lack of control over key stars and directors brought the studio system down. Bit by bit, the studios closed down various departments. Ray Jones left Universal in 1958 when the Portrait Gallery was eliminated.

After retiring from Universal, Jones went into freelance work. He took portraits at his home gallery in the Hollywood Hills. He also accepted freelance work on major productions. The last film he worked on was Paramount's *Pocket Full of Miracles* in 1961. However, he continued to shoot at his home studio. Jones also gave several lectures at the University of Southern California film school on his approach to photographing movie stars as well as the place of photos in film promotion. He hunted and fished in California's wild places and spent time with his wife, Raella, his son John, and his daughter Joann.

Ray Jones had lived in the Hollywood Hills ever since starting as Universal Stills Chief in 1935. He died of a heart attack in those same hills on April 24, 1975. He lived long enough to see the iconographic portraits he turned out by the thousands begin to be appreciated by collectors and photo historians. In the two decades since his death, the appreciation of the unique bequest of Jones and his colleagues has done nothing but grow. If, during their working lives, studio photographers were, as Jones called them, "the unsung heroes of Hollywood,"[22] times have long changed. The place of the studio portrait photographers in creating and sustaining the myths of the dream factory is secured. Aside from the films themselves, their images have become the enduring form of the Golden Age of Hollywood.

Rhonda Fleming, 1954

1930s

EARLY 1920S PHOTOS were simply composed with flat lighting and soft focus. Clothing was generally demure. Pictorialism, the soft-focus, painterly, "artistic" approach to photography popular since the turn of the century, did not translate to the Hollywood Stills Units. While props remained minimal, in the 1930s the lighting changed radically and the stars' images became overtly sexual. The glamour portraits, nascent in the 1930s and perfected by the '40s, were intended as golden fantasies of perfect people, created by the imagination of the great studio photographers and their army of retouchers: an escape from the Great Depression.

43

Jean Harlow, IRON MAN, *1931*

45

Grace Bradley, 1935

Joan Bennett, MANY A SLIP, *1931*

Deanna Durbin, 1938

Deanna Durbin, 1937

Deanna Durbin (née Edna Mae Durbin) was signed by Universal in 1936, when she was fifteen, after a 6-month stint at MGM which did nothing for her. As a wholesome young lead of the 1930s and '40s, she helped bring the studio back from financial ruin. She starred in 21 films before retiring in 1948, in her mid-twenties. Ray Jones was responsible for delicately transforming her image from child star (see page 18) to young woman. In 1938 she shared a Special Academy Award with Mickey Rooney for "bringing to the screen the spirit and personification of youth."

48   *Deanna Durbin and Robert Stack,* FIRST LOVE, *in which she received her first on-screen kiss, 1939*

Deanna Durbin, transformed here into a mature, sexual being, 1945

51

Wendy Barrie, 1937

Marion Martin, SINNERS IN PARADISE, *1938*   53

This photograph of Marjorie Martin (1939) won the Hollywood Stillsmen Association award for "Best Glamour Portrait." 1939 was the only year the Hollywood Stillsmen Association gave awards; they may have spurred the Academy of Motion Pictures Arts and Sciences to start giving awards to still photographers in 1941.

Sigrid Gurie, date unknown

Marjorie Lord was a sexy pinup favorite who later became television's quintessential mom on THE DANNY THOMAS SHOW *in the 1950s. Here she is in 1938.*

Larry Blake, 1937

Toby Wing, 1934

Irene Dunne, 1937

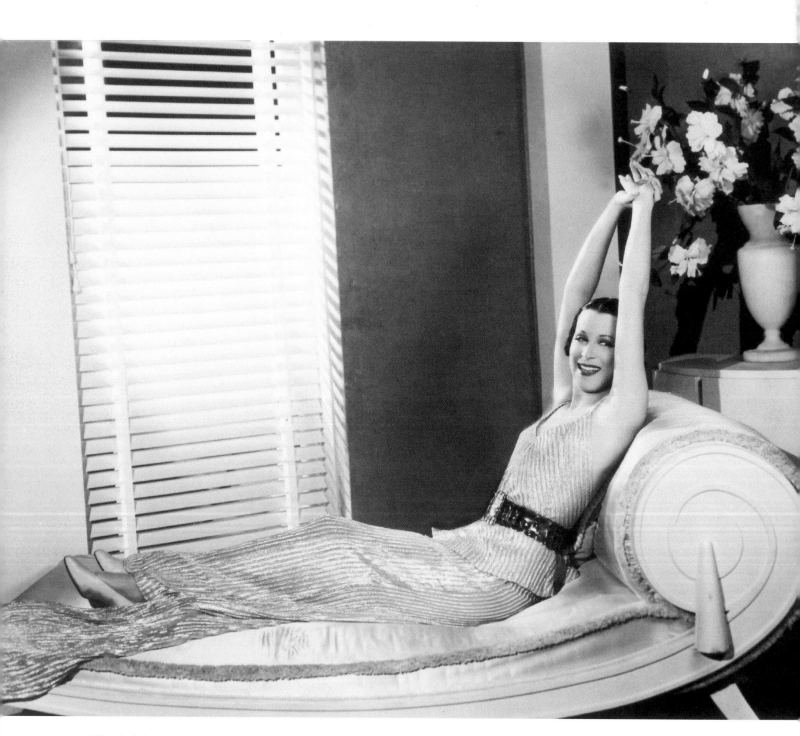

Kitty Carlisle, 1934

Lilian Harvey, MY WEAKNESS, *1935*

Danielle Darrieux, 1938

61

Sir Guy Standing, 1935

Robert and Jackie Coogan, 1931

63

Edgar Bergen, Charlie McCarthy and W.C. Fields, YOU CAN'T CHEAT AN HONEST MAN, *1939*

*Photographed in 1934 during Jones' freelance period, the lavishly
Art Deco* CLEOPATRA *was produced by Cecil B. De Mille for Paramount.*

Claudette Colbert, CLEOPATRA, *1934*

Henry Wilcoxon, CLEOPATRA, *1934*

Claudette Colbert, CLEOPATRA, *1934*

Colbert with a splendid beaded costume; the made-to-look-tough Henry Wilcoxon as Mark Antony

Henry Wilcoxon, 1935　　　　　　　　　　　　　　　*Ken Murray, 1936*

Basil Rathbone, c. 1940

Vincent Price, SERVICE DE LUXE, *1938*

Whenever Jones was asked the name of the most beautiful woman he had ever photographed, he said she was Danielle Darrieux.
Her career in the United States was very brief, but she was a huge star in France. Here she is posed in front of a favorite gallery prop (1938).

19|40s

THE PORTRAITURE so emblematic of the Golden Age of Hollywood emerged as a distinct iconographic style. The new photographic approach featured expressive "Rembrandt" lighting, creating shadows molding the face and body. The introduction of panchromatic film helped produce a fuller tonal range in prints. What emerged was a highly stylized portrait. A larger-than-life image was projected.

Marlene Dietrich, 1941

74   *Marlene Dietrich*, DESTRY RIDES AGAIN, *1939*

Marlene Dietrich and John Wayne, THE SPOILERS, *1942*
Born Maria Magdalene Dietrich in Germany, Marlene studied acting under Max Reinhardt. During the 1920s, she made about a dozen films in Germany before leaving for the U.S. with Josef von Sternberg to make THE BLUE ANGEL *(1930) for Paramount Pictures. The creative collaboration of Miss Dietrich and von Sternberg continued until 1935. During World War II, she made many USO appearances. Her last film appearance was in 1979 with David Bowie in* JUST A GIGOLO.

Randolph Scott, c. 1945

Marlene Dietrich, 1942

Ann Blyth was one of Universal's top stars. She appeared in eighteen movies while under contract.
Here she appears in costume for MR. PEABODY AND THE MERMAID *(1948).*

Merle Oberon, c. 1945

Vera Zorina, 1946

Ilona Massey, c. 1942

Ava Gardner, THE KILLERS, *1946*

82

Wanda Hendrix, 1947

Joan Bennett, 1945

Irene Hervey's photo session with Ray Jones for DESTINATION UNKNOWN *(1942) produced strikingly different moods in the two photographs.*

Mae West, MY LITTLE CHICKADEE, *1940*

87

Maria Montez, WHITE SAVAGE, *1943*

Shelley Winters and Dan Duryea in JOHNNY STOOL PIGEON, *1949;*
Duryea appeared in twenty-five movies from 1945 to 1964

Ava Gardner and Burt Lancaster, THE KILLERS, *1946*

John Barrymore, 1940

Louis Jourdan, 1945

Mischa Auer, c. 1940

Jean Parker, 1944

The master portrait photographers were members of the studio publicity department. A major part of their job was to promote contract players. Holidays were always great occasions to take photos unrelated to any specific film and get them into the newspapers; Jones was a virtuoso of seasonally themed photos. Mindful of the advertising dictum that both men and women prefer to look at photos featuring women, the holiday shots almost always showed the Studio's starlets. In this case, Anne Nagel is furthering her career with a pumpkin at Halloween, 1946.

94

Maureen O'Hara in BAGDAD, *1949*

95

Sabu was discovered by Robert Flaherty while a stable boy at the court of an Indian maharajah. His film debut was the title role in Flaherty's 1937 production of ELEPHANT BOY. *After appearing in several other British films, he went to Hollywood, where he was cast by Universal in exotic roles in a series of popular adventure films, often co-starring Jon Hall and Maria Montez—as he was here in* COBRA WOMAN, *1943.*

1950s

THE POST-WAR STYLE OF PORTRAITURE was considerably different from the iconographic approach. The stars were no longer depicted as deities come to earth, but as ordinary people who just happened to be extraordinarily good-looking. The style of these portraits was modern in its sharp focus. The use of strobes resulted in flat, illuminating light rather than the sculpting light of the 1930s.

Dorothy Malone, LAW & ORDER, *1953*

Jones created both sultry and innocent images of Susan Hayward, 1950s.

Anita Ekberg, a former Miss Sweden who competed in the Miss Universe contest, was under contract to Universal Pictures. This photo is c. 1953.

Tony Curtis, 1950s

Tony Curtis and Janet Leigh, probably during HOUDINI, *1953*

Tony Curtis began his career at Universal in 1949, where he worked steadily for a decade, starting with his screen debut in
CRISS CROSS *(1949) with Burt Lancaster, Yvonne DeCarlo and Dan Duryea; he was in his early twenties at the time.*

Ronald Reagan, 1950s.

105

Rock Hudson, 1950s

John Gavin, BEHIND THE HIGH WALLS, *1956*

Victor Mature and Suzan Ball, CHIEF CRAZY HORSE, *1955*

107

This still of George Nader and Virginia Mayo, from CONGO CROSSING *(1956), shows the typical '50s-style flat lighting and staged appearance.*

Jimmy Stewart, c. 1953

1636·P22

Jimmy Stewart, HARVEY, *1950*

Despite a long-term contract with MGM, James
"Jimmy" Stewart starred in many films away from the
studio. He joined Marlene Dietrich in Universal's
DESTRY RIDES AGAIN *in 1939. In 1952,*
he successfully negotiated the first percentage-basis
contract with Universal, resulting in HARVEY *(1950)*
and a series of Hitchcock thrillers, including REAR
WINDOW *(1954) and* THE MAN WHO KNEW TOO
MUCH *(1956).*

AFTERWORD

In 1975 Ray Jones, a vibrant and dynamic man who appeared in good health, died suddenly. His death was a shock to his family, friends, and associates. Their consolation was that he lived a happy and productive life. He was a good husband and father who loved his family. Ray Jones was a man who cared about people.

Creating this book has been a labor of love. Doing a book about a man—our father—who contributed uniquely to that era with his extraordinary photography of the grand stars has been a remarkable experience.

As you read *Light and Illusion,* what becomes immediately apparent is that much of Jones' success as a portrait photographer was due to the confidence and trust he inspired in his subjects. Sitting in front of a huge portrait camera with a seventeen-inch lens pointed at you, a bank of lights, and technicians running all over can be an intimidating experience even for a trained actor. Under those circumstances, you had better have confidence and trust in the man running the camera.

Nearly a generation has passed since his death. Intermittently over the years my sister, Joann Rickard, and I have been collecting and retrieving his work, which was literally scattered all over the United States and Europe. During an interview session with Robert Stack, Bob happened to mention a Ray Jones picture of him and Deanna Durbin that was on the wall in the attic where Anne Frank was hiding with her family during World War II. She put up pictures of movie stars to make her trapped life a little more comfortable; she liked to collect them. We found out that this picture was on the recreated wall at the Anne Frank Museum in Amsterdam. We got in touch with the museum and requested a copy of the picture, which they promptly sent us.

This was only one of the many fortuities we enjoyed during the retrieval process. When we finally decided to get our book published, we met with a number of agents and publishers and ultimately made contact with Balcony Press, which specializes in Los Angeles architectural and photographic subjects. Balcony Press is owned by Ann Gray, formerly an architect with Paramount Pictures. Balcony has published some of the most beautiful books on architecture and photo-journalistic subjects I have seen. We met with Ann, who instantly fell in love with our project. *Light and Illusion* thus became a reality.

This project has provided my sister and me with a stage on which to bestow a final tribute to our father and his photography. We know you'll enjoy the book.

John Jones and Joann Rickard

Joann Jones Rickard, 1940

Ray couldn't help but make his son, John, look like Ken Maynard or Hoot Gibson when he posed him in his cowboy suit in 1942.

Ray Jones, c. 1958

EDITOR'S ACKNOWLEDGMENT

This book could not have been produced without the help of some very talented people: Tom Zimmerman, our gifted writer/researcher; our publisher, Ann Gray, who simply is Balcony Press. Robert Stack was one of my father's best friends and a great supporter of this project.

My thanks also to the wonderful people who gave of their time in sharing stories and reminiscing about those years: Ann Blyth, Arlene Dahl, Rhonda Fleming, John Gavin, A.C. Lyles, and Hugh O'Brien.

I would also like to acknowledge my wonderful sister, wife and children, who are always there for me with love and support. JJ

AUTHOR'S ACKNOWLEDGEMENT

The staff of the Margaret Herrick Library of the Academy of Motion Picture Arts and Sciences was extremely helpful in tracking down the photographs of Ray Jones and the history of Universal Studios. I particularly want to thank Robert Cushman, Faye Thompson and Sondra Archer of the Special Collections Department. Andy Eskind of the International Museum of Photography at George Eastman House personally searched their extensive Hollywood portrait collection to find those taken by Ray Jones. Bob Cosenza, the manager of the Kobal Collection office in New York, helped to locate the Jones photos in their massive inventory of prints. Marc Wanamaker uncovered several photos of Jones in action in his Bison Archives. Sid Avery shared his intimate knowledge of photography in the Hollywood studio system and the contents of his Motion Picture and Television Photo Archive. Yt Stoker of the Anne Frank Home and Museum in Amsterdam provided the photograph and appropriate diary quotations regarding the elegiac wall. Christina Lake of the Superior Convention and Visitors Bureau and Barry Singer of the Superior Library tracked down information on Ray Jones' life before coming to Hollywood. Director of Photography, David DuBois, instructed me on the wonders of the cucoloris.

Sandy Strick, real estate agent extraordinaire, first introduced me to John Jones. John wanted to do a book to honor his father's talent and took much time from his busy life to answer questions about his family and helped to keep the photos from being a complete homage to Maria Montez. Michael Dawson, third-generation leader of Los Angeles' finest source for all things related to Southern California, Dawson's Bookshop, introduced me to Ann Gray of Balcony Press. She made sure we kept on schedule and helped arrange interviews. Michael John Sullivan was a great source in tracking down information on the stars; he helped me improve the introduction; and he dreamed up the title. TZ

FOOTNOTES

1. Robert Stack, personal interview, March 24, 1997.

2. The Bibliography lists several books about Hollywood stills photography. The best place to start is David Fahey and Linda Rich, *Masters of Starlight* (Los Angeles, California: County Museum of Art, 1987) and John Kobal, *The Art of the Great Hollywood Portrait Photographers* (New York: Knopf, 1980).

3. (New York: Quigley, 1937), unpaginated.

4. Two excellent studies of the studio system are Douglas Gomery, *The Hollywood Studio System* (New York: St. Martin's, 1986), and Thomas Schatz, *The Genius of the System* (New York: Pantheon, 1988). Eileen Bowser, *The Transformation of Cinema* (New York: Scribners, 1990) is a good introduction to the early development of the film industry, while pp 14–19 in Richard Adkins' and Kathleen Conner's "California Booms as Film Locale Capital of the U.S." *Shadowland,* 1 (September, 1991), describe how the film industry came to Los Angeles.

5. Leonard Paige, "He Makes the Stars Shine," *Popular Photography,* 2 (May, 1938), p 25.

6. Group F64 was a loose alliance of photographers congregated around the San Francisco Bay Area. It was most active from 1930–1935. Members included Ansel Adams, Edward Weston, Imogen Cunningham, Sonya Noskowiak, and Willard Van Dyke. The group preached the doctrine of straight, unmanipulated photographs. The camera was the tool of their art and should be used as its nature dictated, not forced to lie by purposely putting it out of focus. The Group's name came from the smallest aperture of the camera lenses then available, F64, which produced the most sharply defined negatives possible.

7. For Steichen's impact, see his *A Life in Photography* (Garden City: Doubleday, 1963) and Christian Petersen, *Steichen: The Portraits* (Minneapolis: Minneapolis Institute of Arts, 1984). Fahey and Rich's *Masters of Starlight* is the best source for quick sketches of Hollywood photographers.

8. Hollywood portrait lighting is covered in Gene Kornmann, *Lighting the Stars* (Hollywood: Korbar, 1938), and especially well in Mark Vieira, *Hurrell's Hollywood Portraits* (New York: Abrams, 1997). For Ray Jones' approach to lighting his subjects, see Stanley Tess, "Portraiture in Hollywood," *American Photography,* 36 (January, 1942), pp 8–11.

9. John Jones had one of the world's great summer jobs. He helped his father at Universal's Stills Department. He remembers the building setup intimately.

10. Harry Friedman Collection, Library of the Academy of Motion Picture Arts and Sciences, Beverly Hills, *Criss Cross* file.

11. Will Jones, "Glamour Picture is Disappointing." This is a postwar column from a Superior, Wisconsin newspaper in the Ray Jones Collection.

12. "Getting Glamour With Your Camera," *Everyweek Magazine* (January 4, 1942), n.p. Both John Gavin and Hugh O'Brien remembered the "one eye" quotation from Jones.

13. Ray Jones, "Jones' People," *International Photographer,* 10 (May, 1938), p 10.

14. Ann Blyth, personal correspondence, January, 1997.

15. Arlene Dahl, personal correspondence, December, 1996.

16. A.C. Lyles, personal correspondence.

17. John Gavin, personal interview, July 10, 1997; Hugh O'Brien, personal interview, February, 17, 1997.

18. Robert Stack, personal interview, March 24, 1997.

19. Yt Stocker of the Anne Frank House in Amsterdam confirmed what the young diarist had hung on her wall in the family's hideaway.

20. Hollywood Studios' Still Photography Exhibit File, Margaret Herrick Library of the Academy of Motion Pictures Arts and Sciences, Beverly Hills; Pierre Norman Sands, *A Historical Study of the Academy of Motion Picture Arts and Sciences* (Dissertation, University of Southern California, 1966), pp 168–169. These awards were commonly mentioned in articles about Jones. As an example, see: "Speaking of Photographs…. These Show Best Pin-Up Photographer's Technique," *Life,* 16 (March 27, 1944), p 19; "Ray Jones: Glamour is His Business," Pageant (November, 1945), p 67.

21. There are two unattributed newspaper articles in the Ray Jones Collection on this visit: Will Jones, "Glamour Picture Is Disappointing," and "Glamour Photographer's Advice to Camera Fan: 'Close One Eye'."

22. Leonard Paige, "He Makes the Stars Shine," *Popular Photography,* 2 (May, 1938), p 24.

INTERVIEWS AND CORRESPONDENCE

Ann Blyth, personal correspondence, January, 1997

Arlene Dahl, personal correspondence, December, 1996

Rhonda Fleming, personal correspondence, August, 1997

John Gavin, interview, July 10, 1997

A.C. Lyles, interview, July 11, 1997

Hugh O'Brien, interview, February 17, 1997

Robert Stack, interview, March 24, 1997

PHOTO CREDITS

All photographs by Ray Jones unless otherwise noted in captions

Anne Frank Home and Museum, Amsterdam, the Netherlands: p 29
Correction to caption: The actor is Louis Howard not Franchot Tone.

Bison Archives, Marc Wanamaker, Los Angeles, California: front flap, pp 18, 22 (bottom photo), 39 (left photo)

International Museum of Photography at George Eastman House, Rochester, New York: cover, pp 16, 21 (bottom photo), 28 (top photo), 45, 50–53, 55–57, 60, 61 (left photo), 62, 67, 68 (left photo), 69, 80, 84–85

Kobal Collection, New York City: pp 43–44, 74, 86–88, 90 (right photo)

Life, Life Magazine ©Time Inc.: p 26

Margaret Herrick Library of the Academy of Motion Picture Arts and Sciences, Beverly Hills, California: back cover, pp 2, 9, 19, 20, 24, 32–33, 35-37, 38, 39 (right photo), 59, 61 (right photo), 65–66, 73, 75–76, 78–79, 82, 89, 90 (left photo), 92, 94–95, 97–99, 101–107, 109

Ray Jones Collection, curated by John Jones, Los Angeles, California: pp 17 (top photo), 22 (top photo), 27 (top photo), 28 (bottom photo), 30, 41, 46–47, 54, 63, 68 (right photo), 77, 83, 91, 108, 111, 112

A.L. Whitey Schafer Foundation, Capistrano Beach, California: p 21

Superior Chamber of Commerce, Superior, Wisconsin: p 13

Tom Zimmerman Collection, Los Angeles, California: pp 10, 14, 15, 17 (bottom photo), 23, 25, 31, 49, 71, 81, 93

Graciously loaned from private collections:
Arlene Dahl: p 40
John Gavin: p 27 (bottom photo)
Robert Stack: pp 6, 48
Patrick Wayne: p 34

BIBLIOGRAPHY

BOOKS

Advertising the Motion Picture (New York: Quigley Publications, 1937).

Bowser, Eileen, *The Transformation of Cinema* (1907–1915) (New York: Scribners, 1990).

Callarman, Barbara Dye, *Photographers of Nineteenth Century Los Angeles County* (Los Angeles: Hacienda Gateway Press, 1993).

DeCordova, Richard, *Picture Personalities* (Chicago: University of Illinois Press, 1990).

Dick, Bernard, *City of Dreams: The Making and Remaking of Universal Pictures* (Lexington: University of Kentucky Press, 1997).

Emotions Made in Hollywood: The Studio Portraits (Zürich, Switzerland: Museum für Gestaltung, 1993).

Engstead, John, *Star Shots: 50 Years of Pictures* (New York: Dutton, 1978).

Fahey, David and Linda Rich, *Masters of Starlight: Photographers in Hollywood* (Los Angeles: Los Angeles County Museum of Art, 1987).

Fiedler, Franz, *Portrait Photography* (Boston: American Photographic Publishing, 1936).

Finler, Joel, *Hollywood Movie Stills: The Golden Age* (London: B.T. Batsford, 1995).

Fitzgerald, Michael, *Universal Pictures: A Panoramic History in Words, Pictures and Filmographies* (New Rochelle: Arlington House, 1977).

Freulich, Roman and Joan Abramson, *Forty Years in Hollywood: Portraits of a Golden Age* (New York: Castle, 1971).

Gomery, Douglas, *The Hollywood Studio System* (New York: St. Martin's Press, 1986).

Hirschorn, Clive, *The Universal Story* (New York: Crown, 1983).

Horak, Jan-Christopher, *Dream Merchants: Making and Selling Films in Hollywood's Golden Age* (Rochester: George Eastman House, 1989).

Kobal, John, *The Art of The Great Hollywood Portrait Photographers* (New York: Knopf, 1980).

Kornmann, Gene, *Lighting the Stars* (Hollywood: Korbar, 1938).

Koszarski, Richard, *Universal Pictures, 65 Years* (New York: Museum of Modern Art, 1977).

Lacy, Madison and Don Morgan, *Hollywood Cheesecake: Sixty Years of America's Favorite Pinups* (New York: Carol, 1981).

Lawton, Richard and Hugo Leckey, *Grand Illusions* (New York: Bonanza Books, 1973).

Longworth, Bert, *Hold Still… Hollywood* (Los Angeles: Ivan Deach, 1937).

Pepper, Terrence and John Kobal, *The Hollywood Photographs of Clarence Sinclair Bull* (New York: Simon & Schuster, 1989).

Peterson, Christian, *Steichen: The Portraits* (Minneapolis: Minneapolis Institute of Arts, 1984).

Sands, Pierre Norman, *An Historical Study of the Academy of Motion Picture Arts and Sciences* (Dissertation, University of Southern California, 1966) (New York: Arno, 1973).

Schatz, Thomas, *The Genius of the System: Hollywood Filmmaking in the Studio Era* (New York: Pantheon, 1988).

Steichen, Edward, *A Life in Photography* (Garden City: Doubleday, 1963).

Stine, Whitney, *The Hurrell Style: 50 Years of Photographing Hollywood* (New York: J. Day, 1976).

Swope, John, *Camera over Hollywood* (New York: Random House, 1939).

Trent, Paul and Richard Lawton, *The Image Makers: Sixty Years of Hollywood Glamour* (New York: McGraw-Hill, 1972).

Vieira, Mark, *Hurrell's Hollywood Portraits: The Chapman Collection* (New York: Abrams, 1997).

Yockelson, Bonnie, *Alfred Cheney Johnston: Women of Talent and Beauty, 1917–1930* (Malvern, Pa.: Charles Isaacs, 1987).

PERIODICALS

Adkins, Richard, Kathleen Conner, "California Booms as Film Locale Capital of the U.S.," *Shadowland,* v.1 (September, 1991), pp 14–19.

Evelove, Alex, "Secrets of the Glamour Boys," *Popular Photography* v.5 (July, 1939), pp 12–13+.

"Getting Glamour With Your Camera," *Everyweek Magazine* (January 4, 1942), pp 6–7.

"The Glamour Merchant," *Milwaukee Journal* (Sunday Magazine), December 14, 1947, p 8.

"Hollywood's Ace Stillmen," *Minicam Photography,* v.5 (July, 1942), pp 56–61.

"Hollywood's Lens Experts Display Their Best Work," *Los Angeles Times,* (May 6, 1942), p II, 1.

"Hollywood Prize Winners," *Popular Photography,* v.7 (July, 1942), pp 42–46.

Jones, Ray, "Jones' People," *International Photographer,* v.10 (May, 1938), pp 9–11.

Paige, Leonard, "He Makes the Stars Shine," *Popular Photography* v.2 (May, 1938), pp 24–26, 117–118.

"Ray Jones… Glamour Is His Business," *Pageant,* November, 1945, pp 66–73.

"Ray Jones Now Dean of Glamour Photographers," *Superior Evening Telegram* (February 23, 1952), p 16.

Soanes, Wood, "'Still' Cameraman Bares Soul," *Oakland Tribune* (February 21, 1945), p C, 6.

"Speaking of Pictures… These Show Best Pin-Up Photographer's Technique," *Life,* v.16 (March 27, 1944), pp 18–20.

Tess, Stanley, "Portraiture in Hollywood," *American Photography,* v.36 (January, 1942), pp 8–11.

"Twice as Good," *Boxoffice,* (April 19, 1941), p 38.

INDEX

118

120